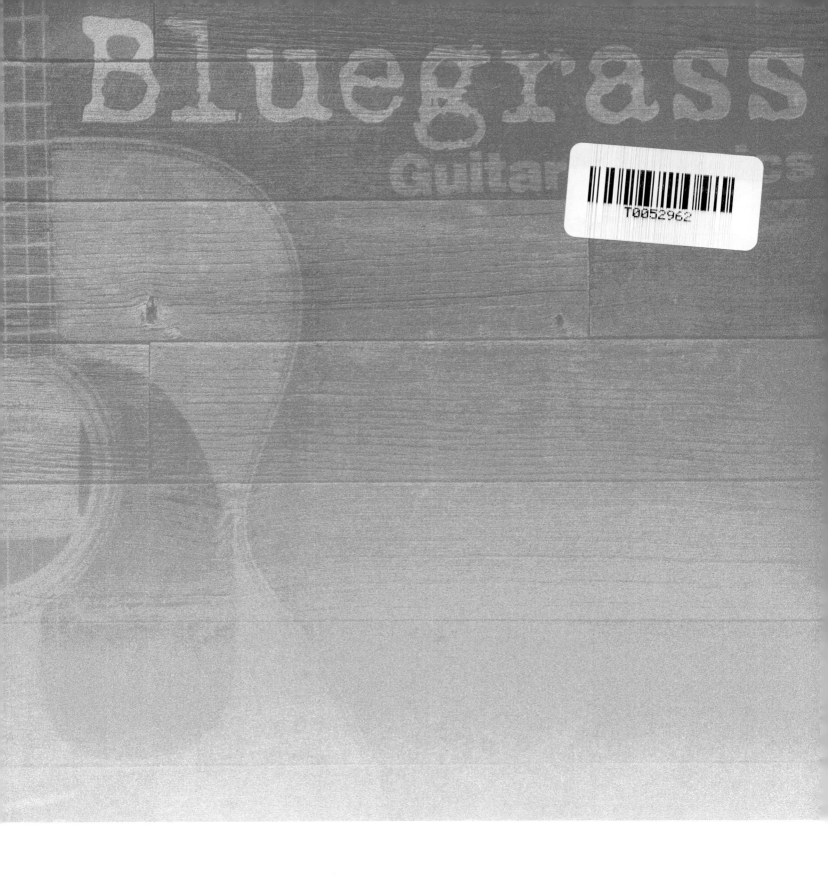

ISBN 978-0-634-04936-1

HAL•LEONARD®
CORPORATION
7777 W. BLUEMOUND RD P.O. BOX 13819 MILWAUKEE. WI 53213

Visit Hal Leonard Online at
www.halleonard.com

Contents

Back Up and Push

Traditional

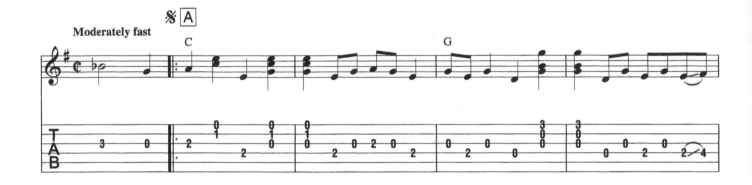

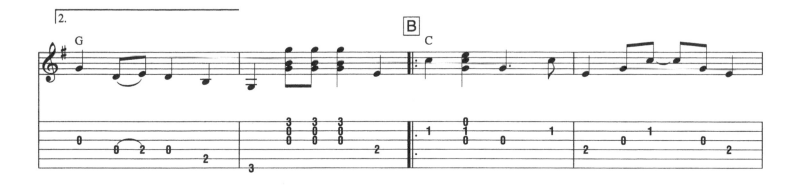

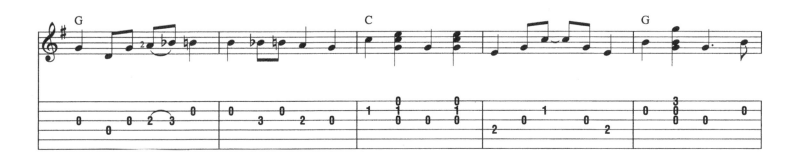

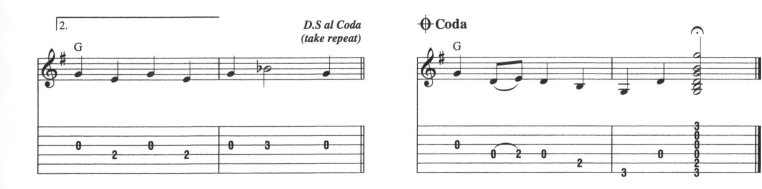

The Big Rock Candy Mountain

Words, Music and Arrangement by Harry K. McClintock

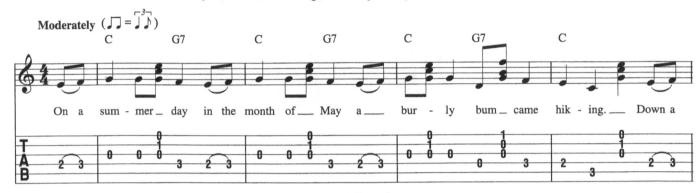

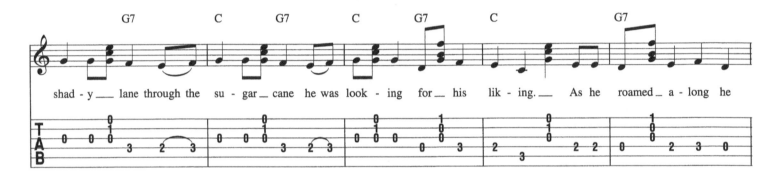

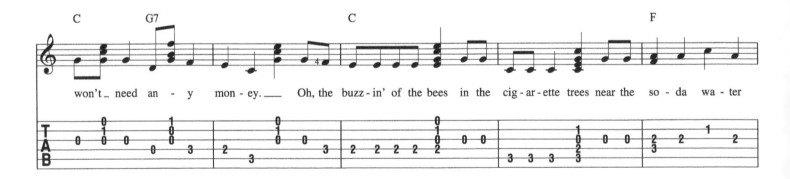

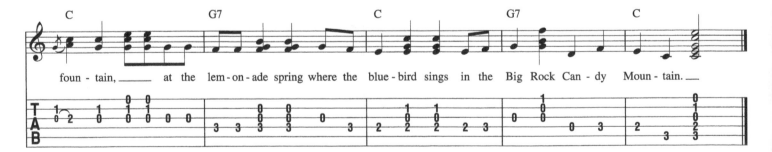

Cotton Eyed Joe

Tennessee Folksong

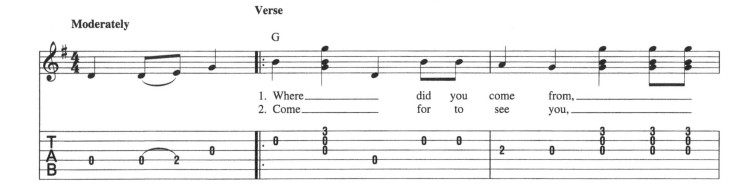

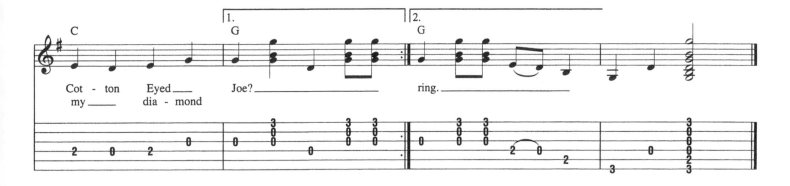

Cumberland Gap

Traditional

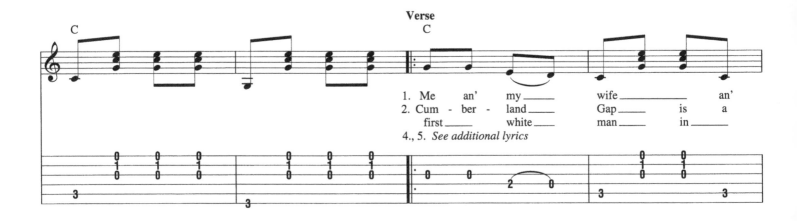

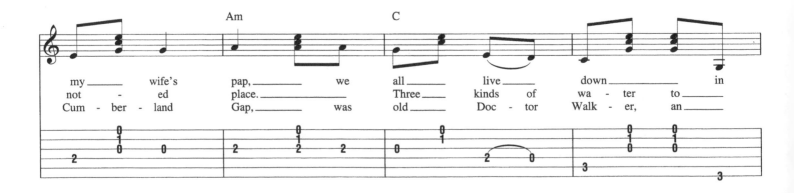

Chorus

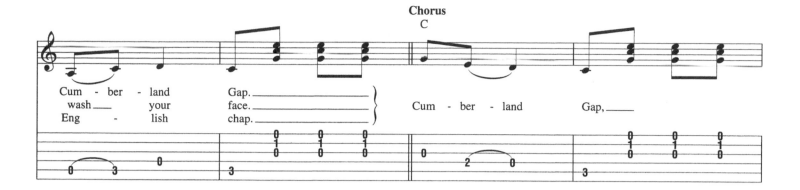

Cum - ber - land Gap. _____
wash ___ your face. _____
Eng - lish chap. _____

Cum - ber - land Gap, _____

Cum - ber - land Gap. _____

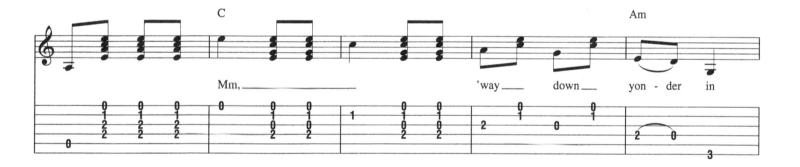

Mm, _____

'way ___ down ___ yon - der in

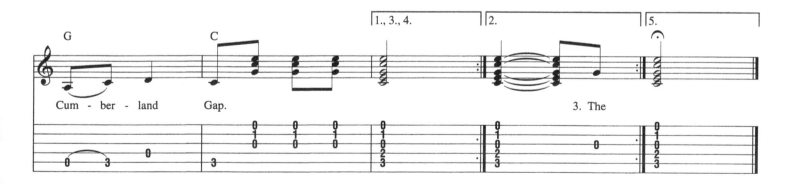

Cum - ber - land Gap.

3. The

Additional lyrics

4. Daniel Boone on Pinnacle Rock,
   He killed Injuns with his old flintlock.

5. Lay down, boys, and take a little nap,
   Fourteen miles to the Cumberland Gap.

Down in the Willow Garden

Traditional

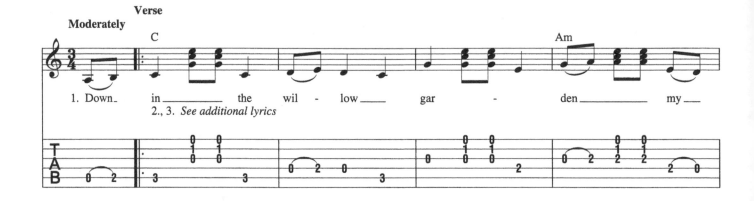

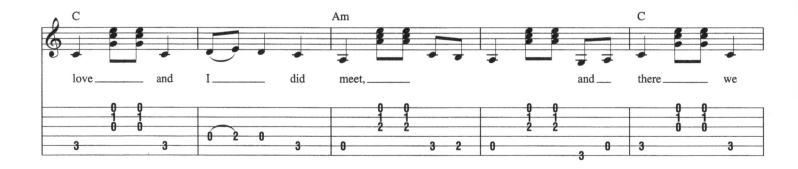

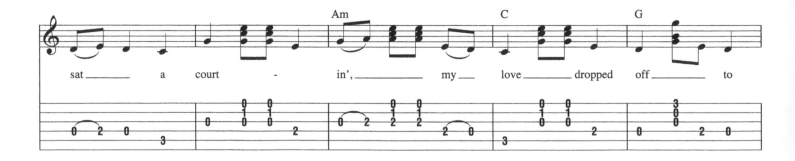

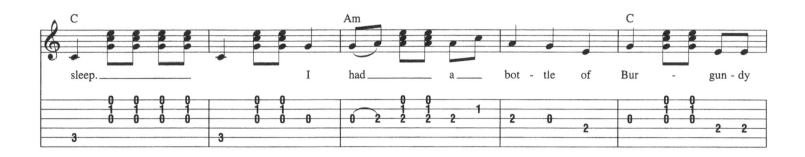

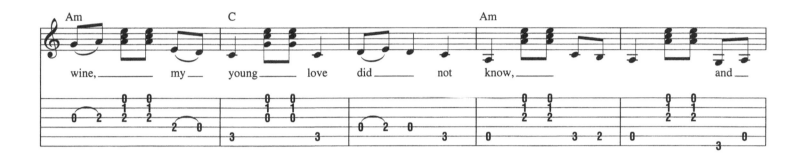

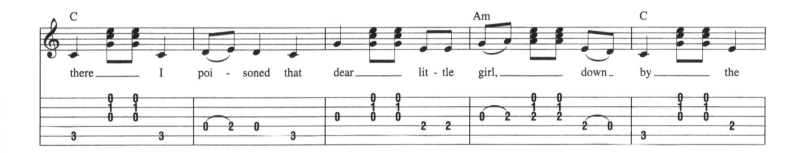

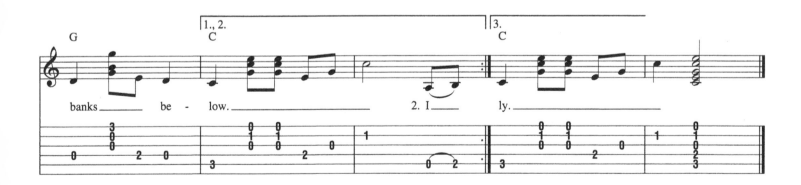

Additional Lyrics

2. I drew my saber through her, which was a bloody knife.
   I threw her in the river, which was an awful sight.
   My father often told me that money would set me free
   If I would murder that dear little girl whose name was Rose Connelly.

3. Now he sits in his cabin door wiping his tear-dimmed eyes,
   Mourning for his only son out on the scaffold high.
   My race is run beneath the sun, the devil is waiting for me,
   For I did murder that dear little girl whose name was Rose Connelly.

Down Yonder

Words and Music by L. Wolfe Gilbert

1., 2. Down____ yon-der some-one beck-ons to me,_____ down____

yon-der some-one reck-ons on me.____ I seem to see a race in

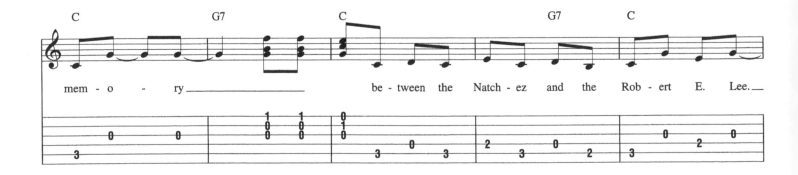

mem-o-ry_____ be-tween the Natch-ez and the Rob-ert E. Lee.____

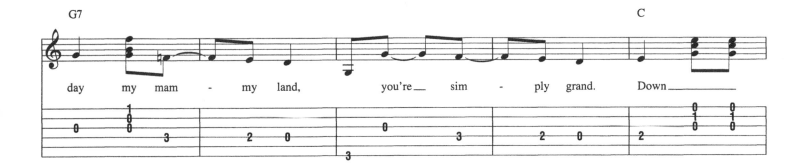

Hand Me Down My Walking Cane

Traditional

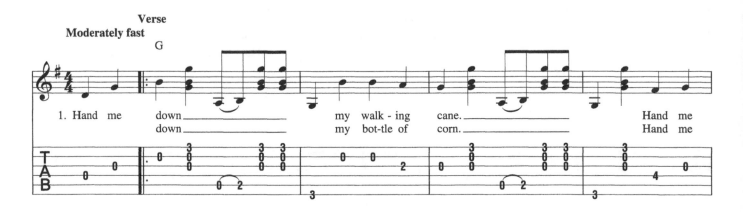

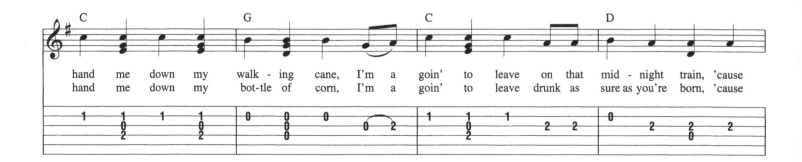

Little Sadie

Traditional

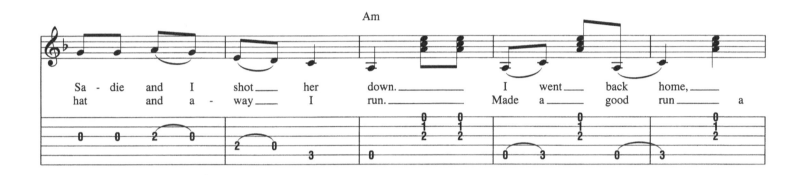

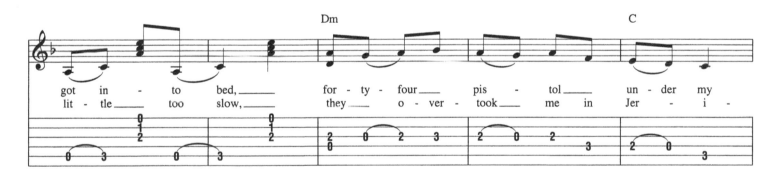

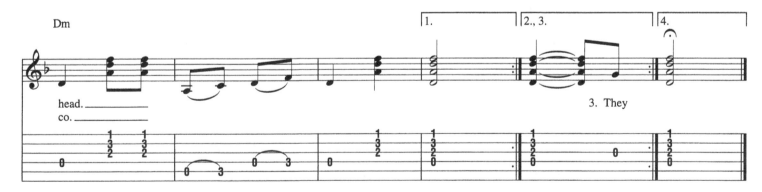

Additional Lyrics

3. They took me down town and dressed me in black.
They put me on the train and started me back.
All the way back to that Thomasville jail,
And I had no money for to go my bail.

4. The judge and the jury, they took their stand.
The judge held the papers in his right hand.
Forty-one days and forty-one nights,
Forty-one years to wear the ball and stripes.

Jesse James

Missouri Folksong

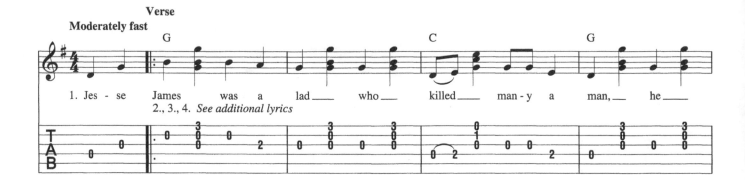

1. Jes - se James was a lad who killed man - y a man, he
2., 3., 4. *See additional lyrics*

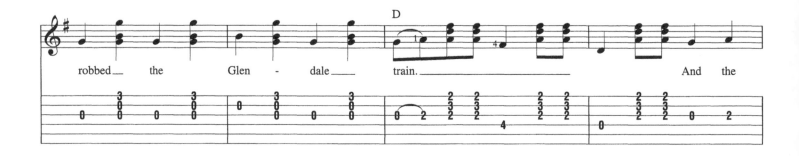

robbed the Glen - dale train. And the

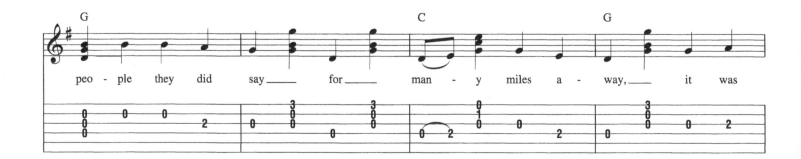

peo - ple they did say for man - y miles a - way, it was

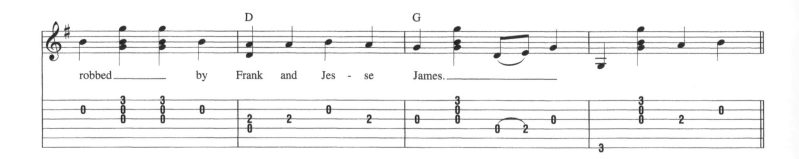

robbed by Frank and Jes - se James.

Chorus

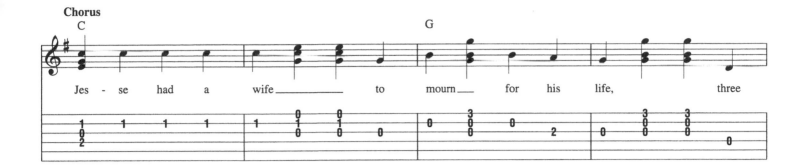

Jes - se had a wife to mourn for his life, three

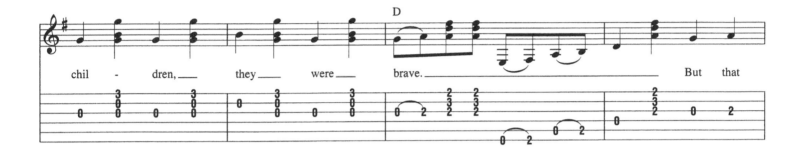

chil - dren, they were brave. But that

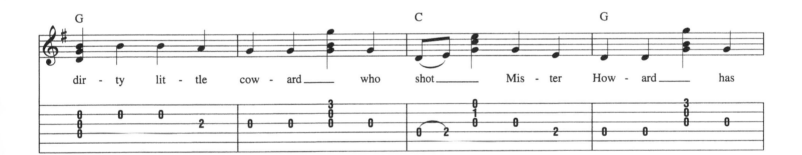

dir - ty lit - tle cow - ard who shot Mis - ter How - ard has

laid poor Jes - se in his grave. 2. It was

Additional Lyrics

2. It was on a Wednesday night, the moon was shining bright,
They robbed the Glendale Train.
And the people they did say for many miles away,
It was robbed by Frank and Jesse James.

3. It was on a Saturday night when Jesse was at home,
Talking with his family brave,
Robert Ford came along like a thief in the night
And laid poor Jesse in his grave.

4. Robert Ford, that dirty little coward,
I wonder how he feels,
For he ate of Jesse's bread and he slept in Jesse's bed
And he laid poor Jesse in his grave.

John Henry

West Virginia Folksong

1. John Hen - ry was a lit - tle ba - by boy, you could
Hen - ry went up on the moun - tain, his
Hen - ry went in - to the tun - nel, had his
4. – 7. *See additional lyrics*

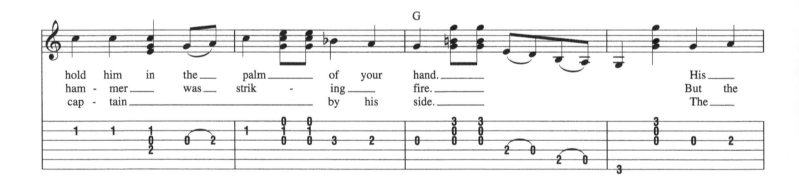

hold him in the palm of your hand. His
ham - mer was strik - ing fire. But the
cap - tain by his side. The

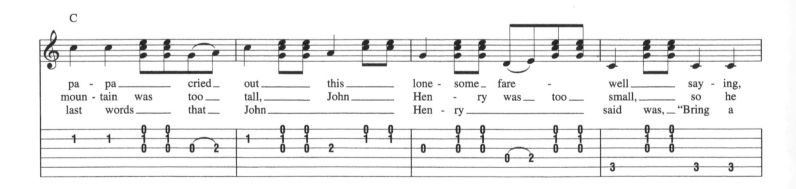

pa - pa cried out this lone - some fare - well say - ing,
moun - tain was too tall, John Hen - ry was too small, so he
last words that John Hen - ry said was, "Bring a

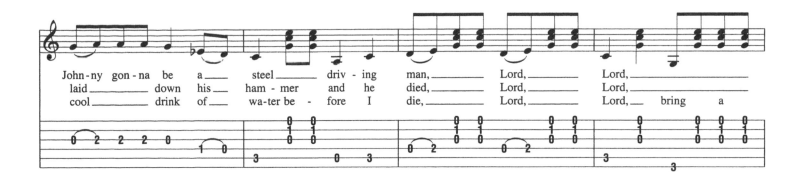

John-ny gon-na be a ___ steel ___ driv - ing man, ___ Lord, ___ Lord, ___
laid ___ down his ___ ham - mer and he died, ___ Lord, ___ Lord, ___
cool ___ drink of ___ wa-ter be - fore I die, ___ Lord, ___ Lord, ___ bring a

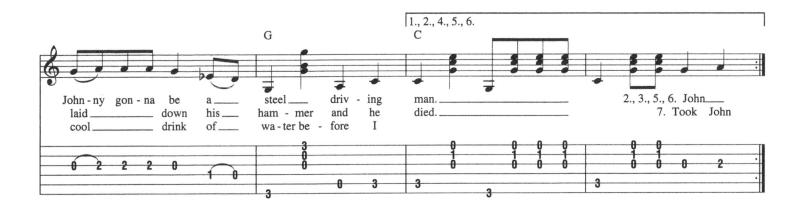

G   C   1., 2., 4., 5., 6.

John-ny gon - na be a ___ steel ___ driv - ing man. ___   2., 3., 5., 6. John ___
laid ___ down his ___ ham - mer and he died. ___   7. Took John
cool ___ drink of ___ wa - ter be - fore I

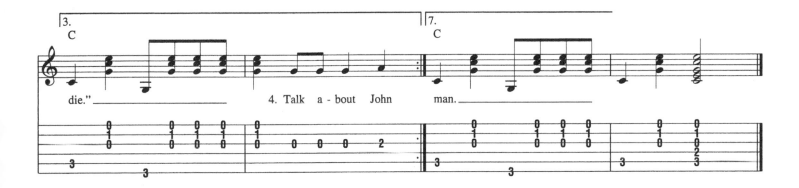

3.   7.
C   C

die."   4. Talk a - bout John   man.

Additional Lyrics

4. Talk about John Henry as much as you please,
   Say and do all that you can.
   There never was born in the United States
   Never such a steel-driving man, Lord, Lord,
   Never such a steel-driving man.

5. John Henry had a little woman
   And her name was Polly Ann.
   John Henry took sick and he had to go to bed.
   Polly drove steel like a man, Lord, Lord,
   Polly drove steel like a man.

6. John Henry told his captain:
   "I want to go to bed.
   Lord, fix me a pallet, I want to lay down
   Got a mighty roaring in my head, Lord, Lord,
   Mighty roaring in my head."

7. Took John Henry to the graveyard
   And they buried him under the sand.
   Now every locomotive comes a roaring by says:
   Yonder lies a steel-driving man, Lord, Lord,
   Yonder lies a steel-driving man.

Long Journey Home

Traditional

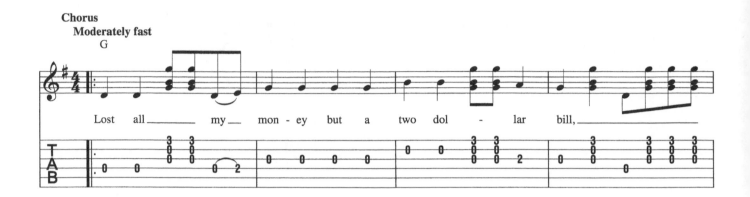

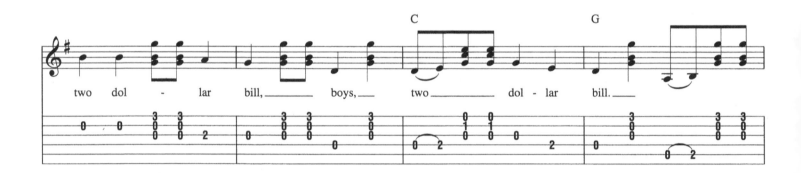

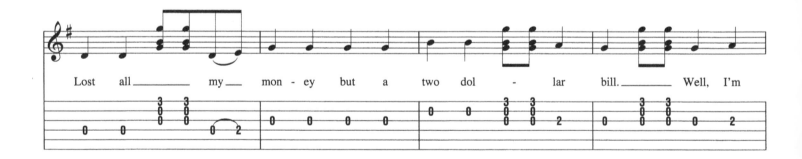

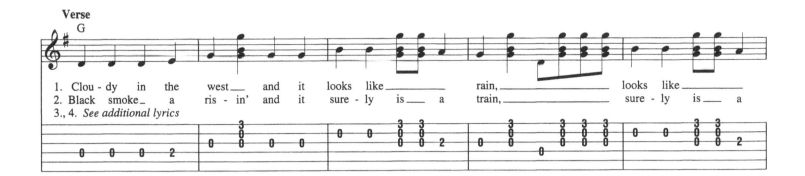

Verse

1. Clou - dy in the west___ and it looks like___ rain,___ looks like___
2. Black smoke_ a ris - in' and it sure - ly is_ a train,___ sure - ly is_ a
3., 4. *See additional lyrics*

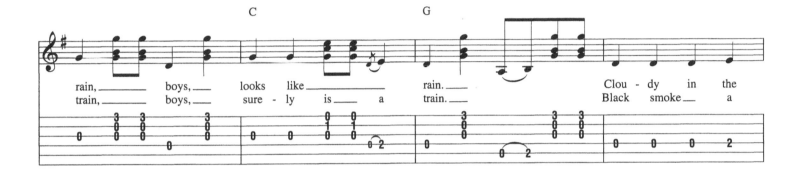

rain,___ boys,___ looks like___ rain.___ Clou - dy in the
train,___ boys,___ sure - ly is_ a train.___ Black smoke_ a

west___ and it looks like___ rain.___ Well, I'm on___ my___
ris - in'___ and it sure - ly is_ a train.___ Well, I'm on___ my___

long___ jour - ney home.___
long___ jour - ney home.___
home.___

Additional Lyrics

3. Homesick and lonesome and I'm feeling kind of blue,
   Feeling kind of blue, boys, feeling kind of blue.
   Homesick and lonesome and I'm feeling kind of blue.
   Well, I'm on my long journey home.

4. Starting into raining and I've got to go home,
   Got to go home, boys, got to go home.
   Starting into raining and I got to go home.
   Well, I'm on my long journey home.

Man of Constant Sorrow

Traditional

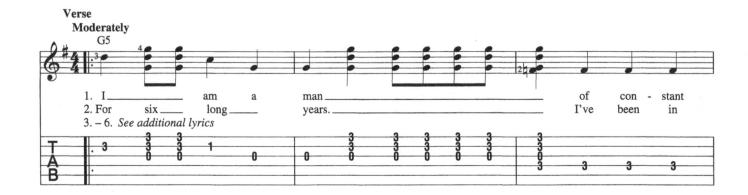

1. I _____ am a man _____ of con - stant
2. For six ___ long ___ years. _____ I've been in

3. – 6. *See additional lyrics*

sor - row. _____ I've seen trou -
trou - ble. _____ No pleas - ure here _____

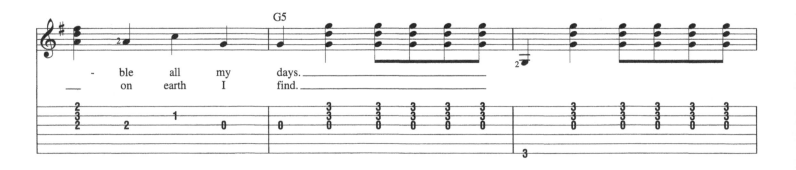

- ble all my days. _____
___ on earth I find. _____

I ___ bid fare - well ___ to old Ken -
For ___ in this world ___ I'm bound to

tuck - y, ___ the state where I ___
ram - ble, ___ I have no friends ___

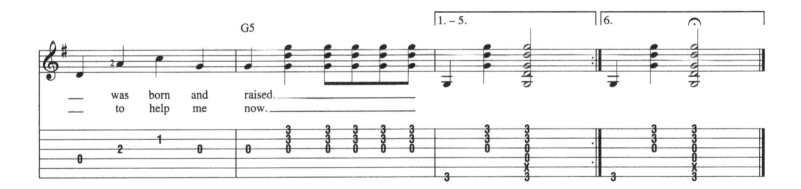

__ was born and raised. ___
__ to help me now. ___

Additional Lyrics

3. It's fare thee well my own true lover.
   I never expect to see you again.
   For I'm bound to ride that northern railroad,
   Perhaps I'll die upon this train.

4. You can bury me in some deep valley,
   For many years where I may lay.
   Then you may learn to love another
   While I am sleeping in my grave.

5. It's fare you well to a native country,
   The places I have loved so well.
   For I have seen all kinds of trouble;
   In this cruel world, no tongue can tell.

6. Maybe your friends think I'm just a stranger.
   My face you'll never see no more.
   But there is one promise that is given:
   I'll meet you on God's golden shore.

Midnight Special

Railroad Song

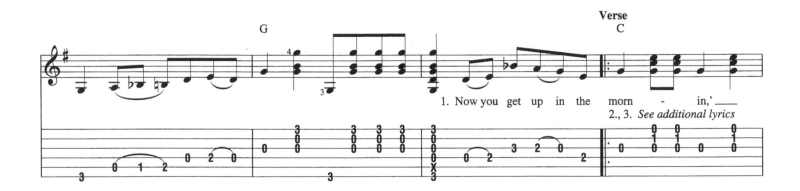

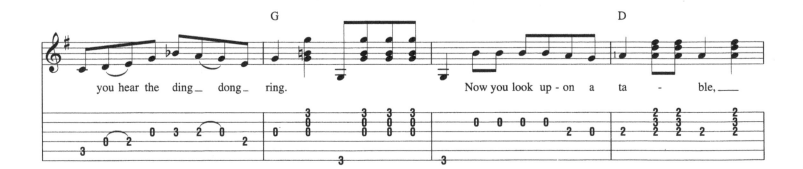

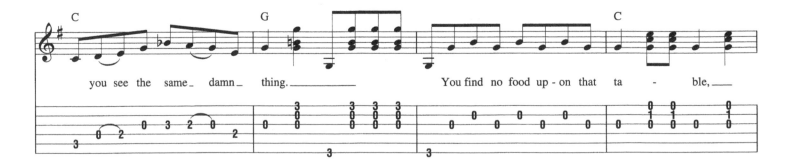

Chorus

Additional Lyrics

2. Well, if you're ever in Houston,
You'd better walk on by.
Oh, you'd better not gamble, boy,
I say you'd better not fight.
Well now, the sheriff, he'll grab you
And his boys will pull you down.
And then before you know it
You're penitentiary-bound.

3. Here comes Miss Lucy.
How in the world do you know?
I know by her apron
And by the dress she wore.
An umbrella on her shoulder,
A piece of paper in her hand,
She gonna see the sheriff
To try to free her man.

Mule Skinner Blues

Traditional

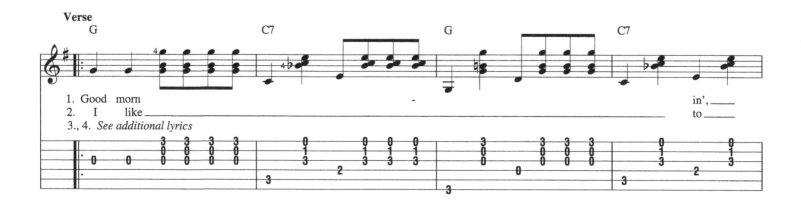

1. Good morn - in', _____
2. I like _____ to _____
3., 4. *See additional lyrics*

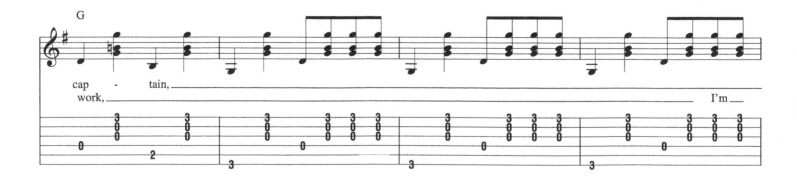

cap - tain, _____
work, _____ I'm _____

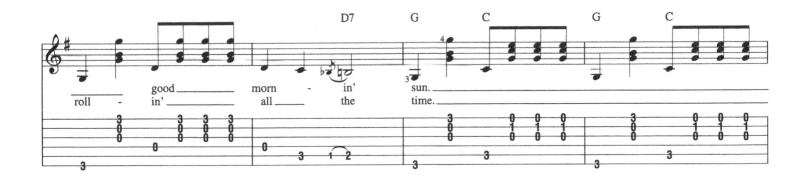

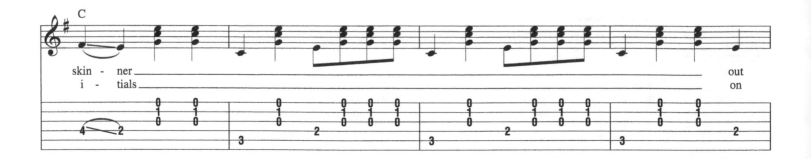

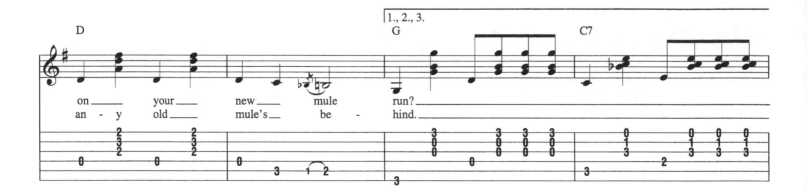

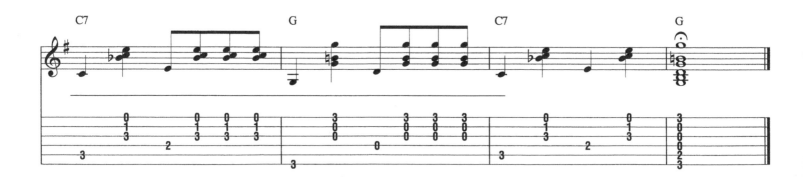

Additional Lyrics

3. Hey there, lil' water boy,
   Bring your bucket 'round.
   Oh well, it's hey there, lil' water boy,
   Bring your bucket 'round.
   If you don't like your job,
   Better lay that bucket down.

4. Workin' on the new road,
   Dollar and a dime a day.
   Oh well, I'm workin' on the new road,
   Dollar and a dime a day.
   I got sixteen women
   Waitin' for to get my pay.

Red Wing

Words by Thurland Chattaway
Music by Kerry Mills

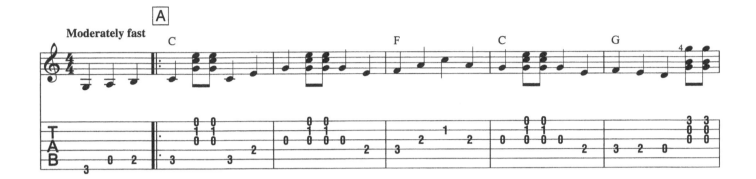

New River Train

Traditional

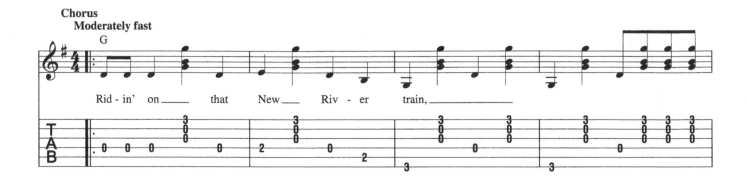

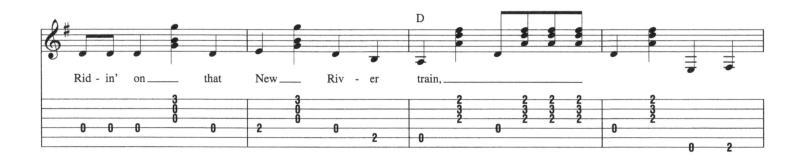

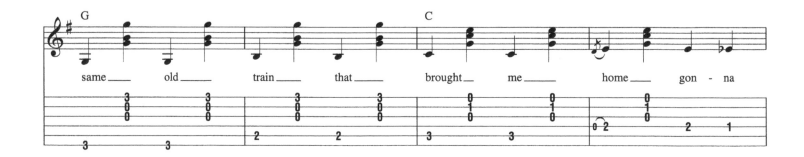

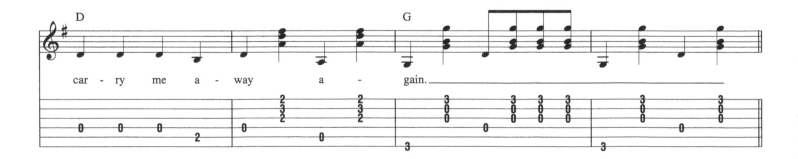

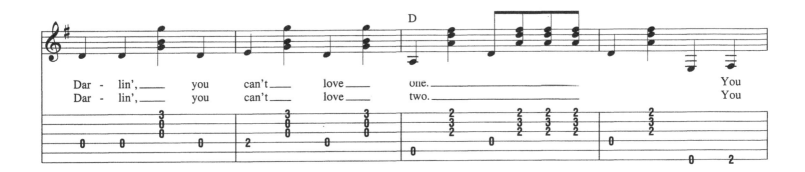

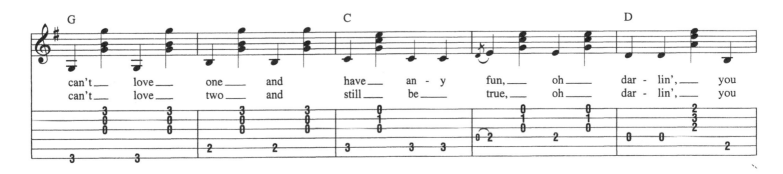

Additional Lyrics

3. Darlin', you can't love three.
   Darlin', you can't love three.
   You can't love three and still love me,
   Oh darlin', you can't love three.

4. You can't love four and love any more...

5. You can't love five and get money from my hive...

6. You can't love six, for that kind of love don't mix...

Roll in My Sweet Baby's Arms

Traditional

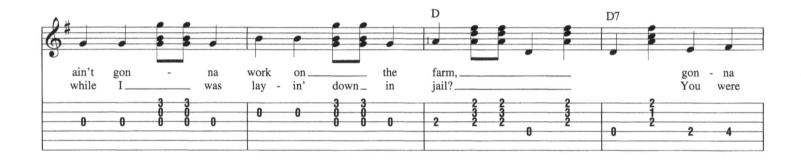

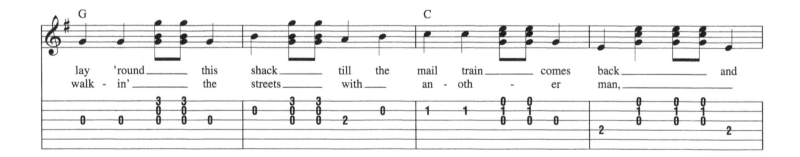

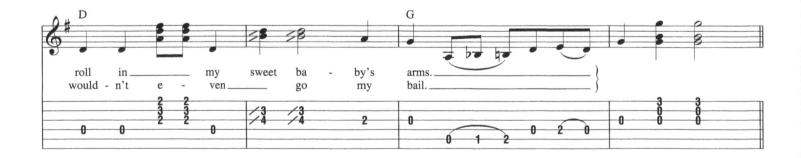

Chorus

Roll in ____ my sweet ba - by's arms. ____

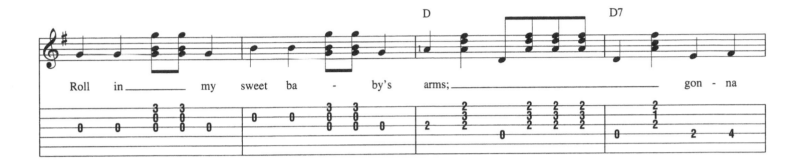

Roll in ____ my sweet ba - by's arms; ____ gon - na

lay 'round ____ this shack ____ till the mail train ____ comes back ____ and

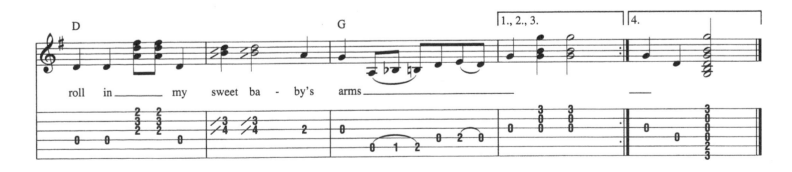

roll in ____ my sweet ba - by's arms ____

Additional Lyrics

3. Mama was a beauty operator,
   Sister could weave and spin,
   Daddy's got an interest in an old cotton mill
   Watch that money roll in.

4. I know your parents don't like me,
   They run me away from your door.
   If I had my life to live over again
   I wouldn't go back there no more.

Shady Grove

Traditional

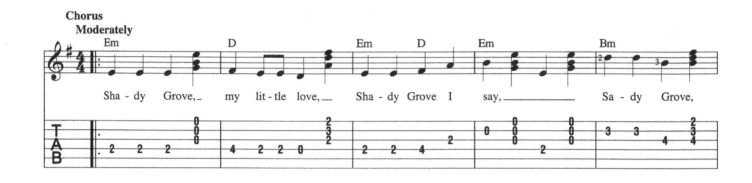

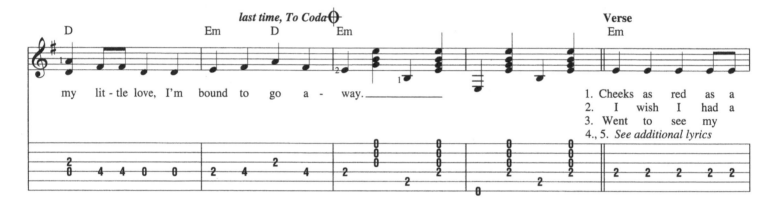

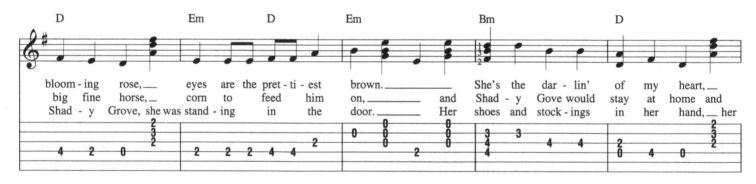

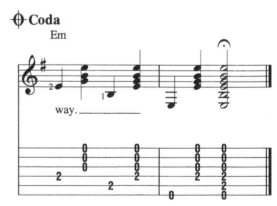

Additional Lyrics

4. When I was a little boy,
   I wanted a barlow knife.
   Now I want little Shady Grove
   To say she'll be my wife.

5. A kiss from pretty little Shady Grove
   Is sweet as brandy wine.
   There ain't no girl in this old world
   That's prettier than mine.

Uncle Joe

Traditional

Additional Lyrics

3. Is your horse a single-footer... *etc.*   4. Would you rather ride a pacer... *etc.*

Under the Double Eagle

By J.F. Wagner

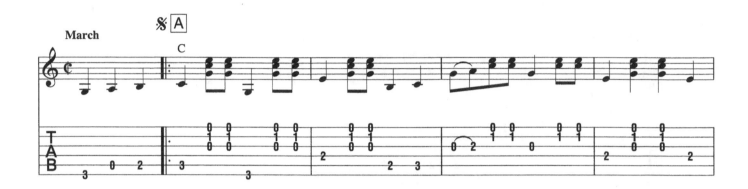

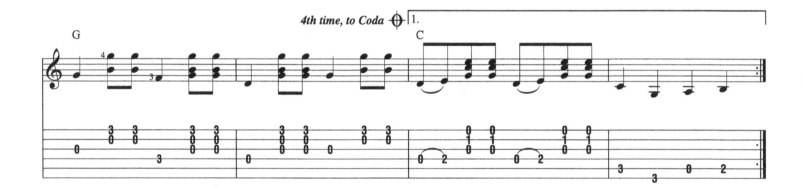

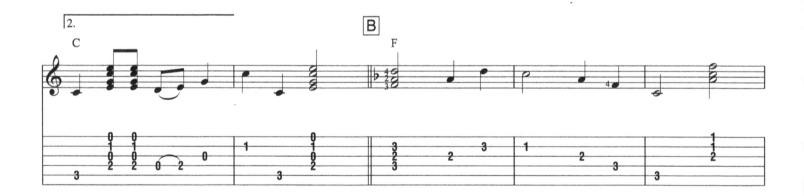

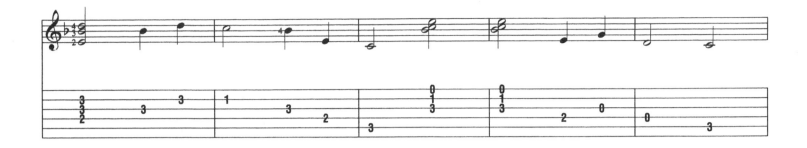

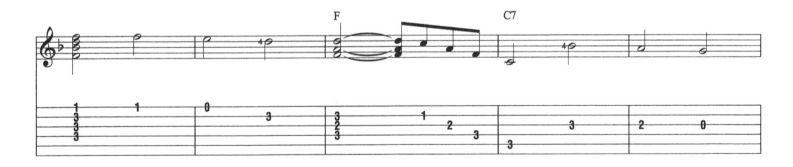

D.S. al Coda
(take repeat)

⊕ **Coda**

The Wabash Cannon Ball

Hobo Song

*T = Thumb on 6th string

Additional Lyrics

3. She came down from Birmingham on cold December day.
   As she pulled into the station, you could hear all the people say:
   Here's a gal from Tennessee, she's long and she's tall.
   She came down to Birmingham on the Wabash Cannonball.

4. Here's to Daddy Claxton, may his name forever stand,
   And always be remembered in the courts throughout the land.
   His earthly days are over and the curtains around him fall;
   They'll carry him home to victory on the Wabash Cannonball.

Wildwood Flower

Traditional

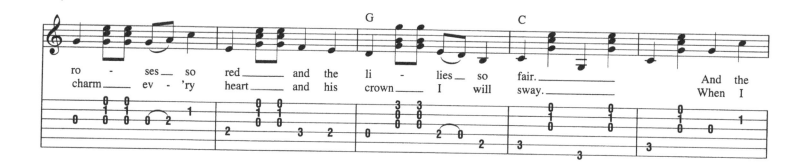

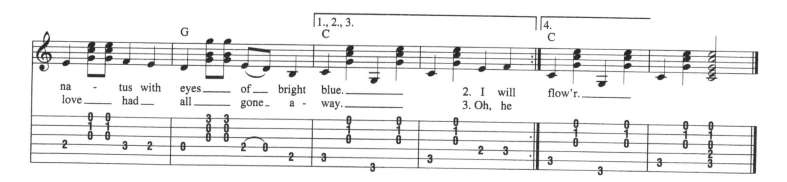

Additional Lyrics

3. Oh, he taught me to love him and promise to love
Through ill and misfortune all others above.
How my heart is now wondering no misery can tell;
He's left me no warning, no word of farewell.

4. Oh, he taught me to love him, he called me his flower
That was blooming to cheer him through life's dreary hour.
Oh, I longed to see him and regret the dark hour;
He's gone and neglected this pale wildwood flower.

FINGERPICKING GUITAR BOOKS

Hone your fingerpicking skills with these great songbooks featuring solo guitar arrangements in standard notation and tablature. The arrangements in these books are carefully written for intermediate-level guitarists. Each song combines melody and harmony in one superb guitar fingerpicking arrangement. Each book also includes an introduction to basic fingerstyle guitar.

 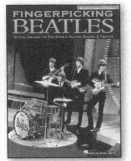    

Fingerpicking Acoustic
00699614 15 songs......................$14.99

Fingerpicking Acoustic Classics
00160211 15 songs......................$16.99

Fingerpicking Acoustic Hits
00160202 15 songs......................$12.99

Fingerpicking Acoustic Rock
00699764 14 songs......................$14.99

Fingerpicking Ballads
00699717 15 songs......................$14.99

Fingerpicking Beatles
00699049 30 songs......................$24.99

Fingerpicking Beethoven
00702390 15 pieces.....................$10.99

Fingerpicking Blues
00701277 15 songs $10.99

Fingerpicking Broadway Favorites
00699843 15 songs......................$9.99

Fingerpicking Broadway Hits
00699838 15 songs......................$7.99

Fingerpicking Campfire
00275964 15 songs......................$12.99

Fingerpicking Celtic Folk
00701148 15 songs......................$10.99

Fingerpicking Children's Songs
00699712 15 songs......................$9.99

Fingerpicking Christian
00701076 15 songs......................$12.99

Fingerpicking Christmas
00699599 20 carols......................$10.99

Fingerpicking Christmas Classics
00701695 15 songs......................$7.99

Fingerpicking Christmas Songs
00171333 15 songs......................$10.99

Fingerpicking Classical
00699620 15 pieces.....................$10.99

Fingerpicking Country
00699687 17 songs......................$12.99

Fingerpicking Disney
00699711 15 songs......................$16.99

Fingerpicking Early Jazz Standards
00276565 15 songs $12.99

Fingerpicking Duke Ellington
00699845 15 songs......................$9.99

Fingerpicking Enya
00701161 15 songs......................$16.99

Fingerpicking Film Score Music
00160143 15 songs......................$12.99

Fingerpicking Gospel
00701059 15 songs......................$9.99

Fingerpicking Hit Songs
00160195 15 songs......................$12.99

Fingerpicking Hymns
00699688 15 hymns $12.99

Fingerpicking Irish Songs
00701965 15 songs......................$10.99

Fingerpicking Italian Songs
00159778 15 songs......................$12.99

Fingerpicking Jazz Favorites
00699844 15 songs......................$12.99

Fingerpicking Jazz Standards
00699840 15 songs......................$10.99

Fingerpicking Elton John
00237495 15 songs......................$14.99

Fingerpicking Latin Favorites
00699842 15 songs......................$12.99

Fingerpicking Latin Standards
00699837 15 songs......................$15.99

Fingerpicking Andrew Lloyd Webber
00699839 14 songs......................$16.99

Fingerpicking Love Songs
00699841 15 songs......................$14.99

Fingerpicking Love Standards
00699836 15 songs $9.99

Fingerpicking Lullabyes
00701276 16 songs......................$9.99

Fingerpicking Movie Music
00699919 15 songs......................$14.99

Fingerpicking Mozart
00699794 15 pieces.....................$9.99

Fingerpicking Pop
00699615 15 songs......................$14.99

Fingerpicking Popular Hits
00139079 14 songs......................$12.99

Fingerpicking Praise
00699714 15 songs......................$14.99

Fingerpicking Rock
00699716 15 songs......................$14.99

Fingerpicking Standards
00699613 17 songs......................$14.99

Fingerpicking Wedding
00699637 15 songs......................$10.99

Fingerpicking Worship
00700554 15 songs......................$14.99

Fingerpicking Neil Young – Greatest Hits
00700134 16 songs......................$16.99

Fingerpicking Yuletide
00699654 16 songs......................$12.99

HAL•LEONARD®

Order these and more great publications from your favorite music retailer at
halleonard.com

Prices, contents and availability subject to change without notice.